MW01014718

LITTLE DEUCE
Coupe

ROBERT GENAT

MBI Publishing Company

To Bill Pitts for keeping the vintage front-motor dragster
flame burning brightly, and for being a good friend

. . . .

First published in 2002 by MBI Publishing Company,
Galtier Plaza, Suite 200, 380 Jackson Street, St. Paul, MN
55101-3885 USA

MBI Publishing Company books are also available at
discounts in bulk quantity for industrial or sales-
promotional use. For details write to Special Sales Manager
at Motorbooks International Wholesalers & Distributors,
Galtier Plaza, Suite 200, 380 Jackson Street, St. Paul, MN
55101-3885 USA.

Library of Congress Cataloging-in-Publication Data
Available

ISBN 0-7603-1106-4

Edited by Amy Glaser
Designed by Alex Perfetti

On the front cover: The 1932 Ford was the first, low-cost
production car with a V-8 engine. It was also the first year
Ford offered two different coupe body styles, a five-window
and a three-window. This chopped three-window highboy,
owned by Bruce Meyer, has been built in the style of a
1950s hot rod, complete with a rare Ardun conversion.

On the frontispiece: This simple V-8 emblem first
appeared in 1932 on the center of the headlight bar on
Ford passenger cars. It was the only indication that the car
was powered by Ford's new V-8 engine.

On the title page: Two friends, two black deuce coupes,
two different styles. In the foreground is Gary Moline's
flathead-powered, chopped fiberglass three-window
highboy. In the background is Michael "Sparky" Spark's
Chevy-powered, full-fendered, unchopped, all-steel
five-window.

On the table of contents page: Deuce coupe owners have
two distinct ways of building America's favorite hot rod—
with or without fenders. The fenders Ford designed for its
'32 Fords were gracefully curved and blended well with the
styling of the body.

On the back cover: The Petersen Automotive Museum in
Los Angeles is home to several hot rods including this
full-fendered '32 three-window owned by Bruce Meyer.
It's been chopped and has an outstanding set of flames.
David Newhardt

Author Bio: Author and photographer Robert Genat has
written more than 20 books for MBI Publishing, which
includes American Drag Racing and the American Car
Dealership. Genat owns and operates Zone Five Photo.
He and his wife Robin live in Encinitas, California.

Printed in China

Contents

Acknowledgments

Hot rodders, and especially deuce coupe owners, are the greatest group of guys in the world. The following '32 Ford coupe owners bent over backward to help me while I was photographing their cars, and they all have subsequently become friends. My thanks to Arden Honrud, Bill Lewis, Rick Cronin, Curt Catallo, George Stupar, John Bade, Mike Martin, Rick Figari, Alex "Axle" Idzardi, Aaron Kahan, Brent Bell, Bill Webb, Richard Lux, Jeff Vodden, Shaun Price, Gary Moline, Mike "Sparky" Sparks, Bob Berry, Sam Davis, Don Garlits, Bruce Meyer, John Guilmet, Garry Biddinger and Howard Gribble (whom I first saw on the San Diego freeway and chased for 40 miles before I could get him to pull over). Thanks to three gearheads who helped me with this book, Gary Jankowski, Gordie Craig, and Dan Burger. Thanks to my San Francisco "transportation captain," Creighton Laskey. A big thanks to Tony Thacker and the staff at the So-Cal Speed Shop and Darin Bond at Gibbon. And thanks to my friend David Newhardt for his excellent deuce photos.

One of my most memorable moments while producing this book was the time I met up with Rick Figari, owner of the yellow '32 five-window coupe used in the movie *American Graffiti*. We had arranged to meet in a parking lot near the Presidio in San Francisco. I was looking for an enclosed car trailer. As if on cue, I saw the yellow '32 coupe emerge from the fog and round the corner in my direction. Figari was tooling around in the most famous '32 coupe to ever grace the silver screen. Like a thousand other guys, I've had a love affair with this car since 1973. When I saw it in person, I had the thrill you get when you meet a sports or entertainment personality you've always admired. As with most personalities, the coupe looked better in person—and unlike a movie starlet, this one gets better with age.

Introduction

It was a bold move, but Henry Ford had a habit of making bold moves. As the Depression was tightening its hold on the nation's financial neck, Ford decided to introduce a new car. It was a new, inexpensive car with a V-8 engine. The new car and engine would cost the company a lot of money, but this project would keep most of Ford's workforce in place. Henry Ford didn't seem to care about spending the money, because he had it in the bank. He was more concerned about keeping the economy going and trying to regain the sales lead from Chevrolet. Ford felt that losing money in the stock market was a greater setback than losing money in the course of running a business. By manufacturing a new car, his workers would at least get paid a salary and would keep the economy going.

Throughout the 1920s, Ford had a successful run with the Model T and subsequent Model A. Henry Ford grudgingly added colors to the Model A, but kept the four-cylinder engine. In 1932 he would introduce a V-8 to one-up Chevrolet's six. At that time, V-8 engines were only installed in more expensive luxury cars. The cost to produce a V-8 was high. Ford didn't copy a design already in production, but designed an entirely new engine with a block that was cast as a single element. This design reduced the manufacturing cost, which made it practical for production. The fact that all the raw materials needed to build a car were inexpensive also contributed to the low cost. The cost of steel was at a 20-year low, copper was at a 30-year low, and aluminum had never been cheaper.

When Ford introduced its new car on March 31, 1932, it offered 14 models, including a station wagon, in both Standard and Deluxe trim. The car was a completely new design, rather than a Model A with a facelift. The '32 model was longer and lower than the Model A and had a more streamlined body. The windshield was slanted back at a rakish 10-degree angle and was no longer covered by a visor, a stylish grille shell surrounded the radiator, and the fuel tank was moved from the cowl to the rear of the car. The frame rails were exposed on the sides of the car above the running boards. With the optional V-8, the '32 Ford was fast. Road tests at the time clocked the new V-8 at 16.8 seconds from 0 to 60 miles per hour, with a top speed of 76 miles per hour.

Considering that the nation's economy was suffering through the worst part of the Depression in 1932, the new Fords sold well at slightly over 300,000 units. Sales, however, fell far short of the 1.5 million cars that Ford had predicted. Prices ranged from $410 for the four-cylinder Standard roadster to $650 for the V-8 powered station wagon.

The '32 Ford's classic lines had an enduring quality. The styling was refined, and the stock version of the car

Howard Gribble's chopped three-window high-boy has an aggressive stance due to big 'n' little tires mounted on Halibrand wheels.

was as fast as any other vehicle on the road. It had that un-deniable "something special" that helped make it the fa-vorite of hot rodders. Any Ford produced in 1932 soon came to be known as a "deuce," referring to the "2" in '32.

In the 1940s, the 1932 Ford was an inexpensive used car. For young me returning from the war, turning it into a hot rod was easy. The switch to a later, more powerful flathead was simple. Aftermarket manufacturers were soon making multicarb intakes, high-compression heads, and full-race camshafts for the flathead. In addition, Ford's 1940s-era production cars had upgraded chassis components, such as transmissions, rear ends, and hy-draulic brakes, which were easily swapped to the '32. Dry lakes racers loved the deuce, because it could be easily fieldstripped of fenders and running boards for competi-tion. Drag racers loved the car for the same reasons. On the street, the '32 looked good with or without the orig-inal fenders. For more variety, the bodies could be easily channeled down over the frame rails, and the tops could be chopped.

When the overhead V-8s became popular in the 1950s, hot rodders found that one would easily fit into the '32's ample engine compartment. The flathead soon made way for Chrysler Hemis, small-block Chevys, and Olds Rocket engines. Behind those en-gines were a variety of manual and automatic trans-missions. Plates were added to the inside of the frame rails (boxing) to increase strength to hold the heavier engines. New cross-members were added to support the varied transmissions. As everything automotive improved, so did the deuce.

In the 1970s, the supply of solid deuce bodies and frames was dwindling. The laws of supply and demand took over, and soon several companies were building re-production frames and bodies. The first bodies (roadsters) were crude and often ill proportioned. As the demand rose, several new manufacturers jumped in to build well-engineered chassis and dimensionally accurate bodies that included both styles of coupe. The world's favorite hot rod was again available to the masses.

Today the demand for a deuce-based hot rod is as high as ever. The mystique and charm of the '32 Ford continues today, as the children and grandchildren of original hot rodders experience the same love affair with the deuce. The '32 Ford, in any body style, will always be the quintessential American hot rod.

Chapter 1

The Original Deuce Coupes

Within weeks of its release, early hot rodders saw the potential of the new deuce. Its fresh styling and engine selection quickly made it a favorite. The new '32 featured a well-developed four-cylinder engine that could be easily modified, and a modern V-8 engine. Racers stripped off fenders and headlights in a crude attempt at streamlining to improve their running times at the dry lakes. For a long time, only roadsters were allowed to race on the dry lakes. Following World War II, coupes were allowed to race on the lakes, and '32 three- and five-windows were some of the first to do so. Tops were chopped to reduce drag and the fenders removed, developing the new highboy coupe look would set the standard for hot rod coupes for decades to come.

A small V-8 emblem graced the center of the headlight bar on all V-8-equipped 1932 Fords. All Deluxe models, such as this three-window, were equipped with cowl lights and a chromed windshield frame. The vertical grille bars on all '32s were painted French Gray.

When the new '32 Fords were introduced, there were two coupe models, the five-window Standard (B-45) and the three-window Deluxe (B-520). Each could be ordered with either a four-cylinder engine or the new V-8. The window arrangement of the five-window, called a "four-window" in 1932 sales literature, gave it the look of the Model A coupe, while the three-window had a look all of its own. Art deco was a strong design theme in the early 1930s, and the entire 1932 line, including the two coupes, embodied the art deco style. The bodies were made of steel with inner hardwood reinforcements. A fabric insert was fitted to the center of the roof, because the techniques required to stamp such a deep draw, or impression, into a large roof panel had not yet been developed. Both coupes came with a rear luggage compartment standard. For an additional $25, a two-passenger rumble seat was available in both versions. The rear window on both coupes could be lowered. In addition to excellent ventilation, this feature allowed convenient conversation with rumble seat passengers.

All 1932 Ford five-window coupes were built as Standard models. The Standard came with a black body and could be ordered in several optional colors, such as this Medium Maroon, but the fenders were always painted black. Colored wheels were a $5 extra cost option.

Both coupes rode on the same 106-inch wheelbase frame, which was 2.5 inches longer than the Model A. For 1932, the rear spring mount was positioned 6 inches behind the rear axle. This spaced the springs 112 inches apart. Ford's theory was that the car would ride better with the springs further apart. The wheels on the

'32 Fords were a drop center design with 32 welded spokes. Standard tires were 5.25X18 black sidewalls, with optional white sidewall tires. The front axle was a forged I-beam design supported by a transverse spring with 12 leaves. The rear spring on both coupes had 9 leaves. Mechanically actuated drum brakes were fitted

Both the three- and five-window coupes had a rumble seat for an option. It used the same deck lid as those coupes equipped with a luggage compartment, except it was hinged to open rearward. To facilitate entry to the rumble seat, round rubber step pads were added to the right rear bumper and to the top of the right rear fender. The rear window on all coupes rolled down for ventilation and to allow the front seat passengers to talk to those in the rumble seat.

on all four wheels, and the spare tire was mounted on the rear of the car.

Both the Standard and Deluxe coupes could be ordered as a Model B with the 50-horsepower four-cylinder engine, or as a Model 18, which included the new 65-horsepower V-8. All Model 18s featured a smart V-8

emblem on the center of the headlight bar. The B and 18 were also included as the first digit in the car's vehicle identification number. Behind the engine were a 9-inch diameter clutch and a three-speed manual transmission. Gear ratios were 2.82:1 for first gear, 1.60:1 for second, and 1:1 for third. The standard rear end ratio was 4.11:1.

Thorne Brown mohair was one of the interior materials available on a '32 five-window coupe. The floor covering on Standard coupes was a simple rubber mat. This coupe has been upgraded with a Deluxe-style tapestry carpet.

In 1932 the left taillight was standard and the right light (shown) was optional. Automatic turn signals had yet to be invented.

Early production cars had 4.33:1 rear axles. Ford had been criticized for the Model A's cowl-mounted gas tank. It was deemed dangerous, and passengers were constantly exposed to gasoline fumes. For the 1932 model, the 14-gallon tank was relocated to the rear of the car between the frame rails.

Standard Five-Window Coupe

The five-window coupe was the Standard model. Like all the other Standard models, it was painted entirely black. The body was painted with Pyroxylin lacquer, and the fenders, frame, gas tank, and wheels were dipped and baked with black enamel. For an additional cost, the body and/or wheels could be painted in any of the available 1932 Ford paint schemes. The grille insert on all 1932 Ford passenger cars was painted French Gray.

The five-window coupe seated two comfortably on a full-width (43.5 inches) bench seat. The door openings were rather small, at only 27.8 inches wide, but inside the Standard coupe offered 37 inches of headroom and a

In the 1930s, a lot of speed equipment was available for Ford's four-cylinder engines, and very little was available for the V-8s. Stupar's coupe runs a highly modified Model B engine with a Cragar overhead conversion and a tubular exhaust header. The modifications to Stupar's engine boosted the horsepower from a stock rating of 50 at 2,800 rpm to 86 at 3,200 rpm.

4-Cylinder Engine Specs

BoreXStroke	3.82X4.25	Number of main bearings	3
Cubic inch displacement	195 ci	Pistons	Aluminum alloy
Horsepower	50 at 2,800 rpm	Engine weight with clutch	
Compression ratio	4.6:1	and transmission	464 pounds
Valve arrangement	L in block	Crankcase capacity	5 quarts

Two Winfield downdraft carburetors are mounted on top of a ram's horn aluminum intake manifold. Stupar's modifications to his four-cylinder engine would have allowed it to whip any V-8 in its day.

distance of 18.2 inches from the clutch pedal to the seat. This was more than adequate for any adult in 1932. Added interior appointments included a dome light, sun visors, and a rear window curtain. The interior was upholstered in Diagonal Dash brown mixed cloth or Thorne Brown mohair. The interior window moldings and dash were painted taupe. The only floor covering available on the Standard coupe was a black rubber mat. Safety glass was used in the windshield and was an option for the side and rear windows. The Standard coupe weighed 2,261 pounds with the four-cylinder engine and 2,382 pounds with the V-8. In 1932, a new four-cylinder Model B Standard coupe was priced at $440. The base price for a V-8-powered Model 18 Standard coupe was $490. Total production for the 1932 Standard five-window Ford coupe was 54,107 units.

George Stupar's "Almost" Stock Five-Window

From the outside, George Stupar's coupe looks like a completely stock '32 five-window. It has the optional Medium Maroon paint on the body and wheels, and the optional right-hand taillight. The interior is covered in the original-style brown mohair. When you look closely at this '32 five-window, the subtle modifications make it clear that it is not completely stock.

When Stupar was in high school in 1964, he owned a true 1950s lakes style, Olds-powered five-window. When he sold it in 1980, he came down with a bad case of seller's remorse. The cure was the purchase of this Model B five-window coupe in 1989. It had been stored in a shipping container for over 25 years, and was complete and in excellent shape.

Because of the outstanding condition of this car, Stupar didn't have the heart to cut it up to make a copy of his first '32 coupe. He decided to restore the car to mint condition and do some mild modifications to represent a period-correct, late 1930s-style hot rod. Stupar's magnificent restoration took eight years to complete. The only notable, albeit subtle, exterior modification is the addition of original aftermarket 16-inch diameter Kelsey Hayes bent-spoke wheels. The front tires are 6.00X16, and the rears are 7.00X16, which give the car a gentle rake.

Under the hood, Stupar's coupe sharply deviates from a stock restoration. Instead of installing a modified V-8,

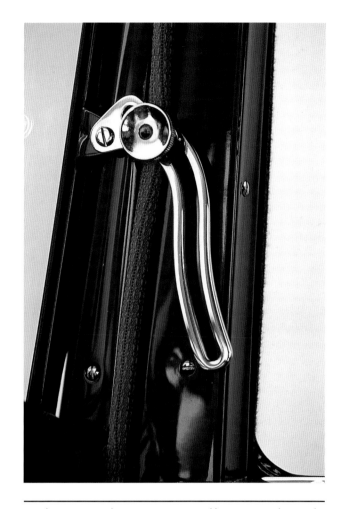

Ventilation was ample in '32 coupes. In addition to a cowl vent, the windshield was hinged at the top and could be tilted out with the help of a pair of windshield swing arms. (Right-hand shown)

V-8 Engine Specs

BoreXStroke	3.06X3.75	Number of main bearings	3
Cubic inch displacement	221 ci	Pistons	Aluminum alloy
Horsepower	65 at 3,400 rpm	Engine weight with clutch	
Compression ratio	5.5:1	and transmission	615 pounds
Valve arrangement	L in block	Crankcase capacity	5 quarts

he chose to hop up the original four-cylinder engine. Using a period-correct Cragar overhead valve conversion, Stupar sharply bumped the horsepower and underhood visual appeal. In addition to the Cragar cylinder head, Stupar added a balanced truck crank, along with a Harman Speed camshaft. The new head increased the compression from the stock ratio of 4.6:1 to a healthy 9:1. Additional engine modifications designed for better lubrication include a modified V-8 oil pump, opened-up oil galleys, and drilled journals. A dual ram's horn-shaped Winfield intake manifold mounts a pair of Winfield carburetors. The exhaust is a four-into-one tubular header that has been Jet Hot-coated. Behind the lightened flywheel is a stock 1932 three-speed that drives into a stock 4:11 rear end. The only modifications made to the chassis were the addition of tubular shocks and the installation of hydraulic brakes.

If the clock were turned back to the late 1930s, Stupar's Model B Standard coupe would be considered a "sleeper." Its benign looks betray its potential for speed. With the overhead conversion, it would have been able to dust off all stock V-8s and give a few of the modified V-8s a run for their money.

Arden Honrud's Unrestored Deluxe Three-WindowCoupe

Ford's top-of-the-line coupe in 1932 was the Deluxe three-window. With the exception of the cowl vent door, all of its Murray-built sheet metal was unique and different from any other '32, including the five-window

Ford's Deluxe coupe in 1932 was this sleek three-window model. Except for the cowl vent, there were no interchangeable body parts between the three-window and five-window coupes. This particular three-window is painted Washington Blue with Tacoma Cream wheels and pin striping, a combination that was available on all Deluxe '32s at no extra cost. Like all other '32 Fords, the fenders were black. This particular coupe is an unrestored original model owned by Ardun Honrud.

All 1932 Fords came with a rear-mounted spare tire. The side fender mounts were optional. This one is equipped with the optional chrome cover. The hubcaps on V-8 models were stamped with a V-8 in the center. Four-cylinder hubcaps had a Ford oval in the center.

As a Deluxe model, the three-window coupe could be ordered at no additional cost in body colors of black, Medium Maroon, Brewster Green, Tunis Gray, Old Chester Gray, Washington Blue, or Winter Leaf Brown. Each of these colors was accented with a harmonizing color for the body reveals, and a third color was used for the pinstripe. Wheels painted in Apple Green, Aurora Red, or Tacoma Cream were also a no-cost option on the Deluxe coupe. As with the Standard coupe, Pyroxylin lacquer was used for the body, and enamel was used for all other exterior components.

Three-window '32 coupes were equipped with rear-hinged doors, known as "suicide doors." Honrud's unrestored coupe still has the factory running board cover, which shows wear spots where the original owner pivoted her foot upon entering and exiting her stylish coupe. The area between the body and running board is the exposed frame rail.

coupe. It featured two large 41.8-inch-wide passenger doors that were hinged at the rear for style, and easy entry was a benefit. This rear-hinged door became known as a "suicide door," because if it opened accidentally when the car was in motion, a passenger could be thrown from the vehicle. The Deluxe three-window was the only 1932 Ford model to feature suicide doors, and it was the only one to have front door armrests and a door pull strap. Like the other 1932 Deluxe closed models, the coupe's interior was appointed with a dome light, rear window curtain, glove box, interior sun visors, cigar lighter, ashtray, and attractive tapestry carpet. The dash and interior window frames were painted in a burled woodgrain finish. Upholstery materials included tan broadcloth, Rose Beige mohair, Tan Bedford Cord, or Copra Drab genuine leather. Cowl lights and full safety glass were also standard on the Deluxe coupe.

Suicide doors swing back to allow easy entry to the coupe's interior. These well-worn Mohair seats on Honrud's coupe were stitched in 1932. Deluxe coupes had a glove box on the dash, and an arm rest and pull strap on the doors. The small T-handle behind the seat is the crank for the rear window.

The cost for a '32 Ford Deluxe coupe with a four-cylinder engine was $500, and the Deluxe coupe with a V-8 was $550. Only 1,258 Deluxe coupes were built as four-cylinder Model Bs, while 22,416 of the V-8 Deluxe coupes were produced. All V-8-equipped cars had a stylish V-8 emblem in the center of the headlight bar and embossed on the hubcaps. Four-cylinder Model B hubcaps featured the Ford script embossed within an oval and a plain headlight bar.

Arden Honrud's Deluxe three-window coupe is an un-restored gem. It was originally purchased on January 28, 1933, at Fortner Motors in Los Angeles. It's one of the late production cars, as evidenced by the 25-louver hood and the dipstick on the driver's side of the V-8 engine. The woman who originally bought the car paid $808.68, which included the cost of a spare tire cover, gas, oil, license, taxes, and insurance. The color is Washington Blue, with Tacoma Cream wheels and striping. Other than the wheels and the grille shell, all of the paint is original. There is even a spot worn through the covering on the driver's side running board, where the owner would pivot her foot, entering or exiting the car. The mohair interior is also original. This three-window "time capsule" is not stashed in a museum or in a trailer. Honrud

Ford used 12 different speedometers during the production run of the '32s. Those used on four-cylinder cars topped out at 80 miles per hour, while the ones used on the V-8 equipped models went up to 90. All gauge panels were machined-turned stainless steel.

occasionally drives the coupe, to the delight of his friends and all those who love '32s.

The big news in 1932 was Ford's new V-8, and while the new Fords were attractive and fast, they had more than their share of teething problems. In the initial design, the idea of a center cross-member for the frame was rejected, so the new frame lacked torsional rigidity. During the nine-month production run, Ford made several attempts to reinforce the frame for stability. Dealers were also instructed to add strengthening plates to the frame. (When the new 1933 Ford was introduced, it would feature the center cross-member that the '32 lacked.)

During the first production year, Ford used three different V-8 blocks. The first 2,000 V-8 engines needed to have their camshafts, pushrods, valves, valve guides, and front covers replaced, and the next 2,000 also had to have the front cover replaced. It wasn't until 1934 that all of the V-8 engine's woes would be fixed.

The efficiency of Ford's basic flathead design, despite bugs in the beginning, was to be proven by a 21-year production lifespan.

In addition to the changes in the frame and engine, there were enough other running changes for those who restore 1932 Fords to divide the production into early, mid-, and late models. For instance, Ford used 12 different speedometers on the 1932 models. Two different hoods were used in domestic production; the early one, with 20 louvers, was used on all Model Bs, and the late one had 25 louvers. It would also be possible to see a Standard five-window coupe with Deluxe items, such as a

The rumble seat on '32 coupes was just wide enough for two adults. The comfortable seat was covered in a simulated leather material. With the rear window rolled down, rumble seat passengers could talk to those in the front seat.

This is the V-8 engine that revolutionized the automobile in 1932. It produced 65 horsepower and was able to push a '32 Ford to 76 miles per hour. The basic flathead design would continue to be installed in Ford passenger cars through 1953.

chromed windshield frame, carpeting, and cowl lights. All 1932 Ford bodies had a reinforcement welded to the inside of the cowl so the cowl lights could be mounted. It was a simple task to drill the holes through the outer skin and attach the lights. A tradition as old as the car itself is the addition of over-the-counter parts to accessorize a new car. Selling cars in the middle of the Depression was tough, and dealers would do almost anything for a sale.

A wide variety of factory and dealer options and accessories could be specified for the 1932 Ford. A side-mounted spare tire moved the spare from the rear to one or both front fenders. With the side-mounted spare, a folding rear trunk rack could be ordered. Ford

also provided an optional trunk designed to fit on the rear trunk rack. For an extra $49, a Grigsby-Grunow radio could be added, with the antenna attached to the underside of the drivers side running board. A spotlight, listed as a "sport light," could be added to the drivers side A-pillar. A right-hand side taillight was also available. For those wishing to cover the rear-mounted spare, Ford offered three different spare tire covers.

Up until 1932, Ford's coupes were boxy and limited in performance. With the introduction of the two new coupes and a snappy V-8 in 1932, Ford reestablished itself as the trendsetter for styling and performance in a car for the masses.

Chapter 2

Deuce Coupe Garage

For the past 60 years, backyard garages across the nation have been teeming with hot rod activity. In many of those garages, American skill and ingenuity have been concentrated on '32 deuce coupes. Those fortunate enough to have one of the original deuce coupes have a prize that's coveted by almost everyone in the hot rod world. For the others, a solid fiberglass reproduction of one of the fabled '32 coupes is the basis for a hot rod. Whether it's an original steel car or a quality reproduction, the fun and overall sense of accomplishment of building your own hot rod is as good as it gets.

All it takes to build a deuce coupe is time, energy, space, and money. Once someone decides to build a car, it takes a plan. The plan includes a vision of what the finished product will look like and the finances to fulfill that plan. The vision is important. It determines the theme or

---

Bruce Meyer's garage is every hot rodder's dream—two deuce coupes and a spare flathead engine on a stand. Both '32 three-windows are beautifully detailed highboys. Meyer also has several '32 roadsters and a few historic race cars.

look of the finished car—retro, high tech, or something in between. Mixing themes, such as installing billet wheels on a retro rod, is one of the most serious hot rod *faux pas*. A car the builder saw years ago might determine the theme, or it might be a combination of details from the builder's favorite coupes. The theme will ultimately determine the cost. A full-fendered car with a steel body, independent suspension with lots of chrome, and a high-tech engine and transmission will cost more than a retro-styled highboy with a low-buck painted suspension and a junkyard Chevy small-block. One simple rule to remember is that everything will cost exactly double what you thought it would.

The most difficult aspects of building a hot rod involve choices and decisions. When someone builds a '57 Chevy, the choice of grille, bumpers, and taillights is limited and clear-cut. When building a deuce coupe hot rod, however, the choices are unlimited. Most builders stay with traditional themes to avoid creating something dated that will be out of style in 10 years. Those who venture too far outside the lines of hot rod tradition may be unhappy with the results within a

Above: Lucky five-window deuce coupe owner Garry Biddinger wrenches on the old flathead engine that came with his coupe. The original firewall has been butchered, but excellent steel reproductions are available. Biddinger is building this coupe as a daily driver for his wife, Dorothy. It will replace her 1940 Ford pickup.

Right: Biddinger's 1932 five-window looks rough, but it's actually in good shape. The missing lower trunk panel can be easily fabricated, and the surface rust on the rest of the body can be removed. This former hot rod coupe's steel rear fenders have a telltale imprint where '39 teardrop taillights once resided.

matter of years. It's best to look to the cars that have stood the test of time and use what those builders did as a guide.

Finding a Body

A steel deuce coupe body is a hot rodder's Holy Grail. Chasing down an original steel body can be a daunting and expensive proposition. The days of the $100 deuce body are as distant as a low-fat cheeseburger. Today, a decent steel deuce coupe body for under $10,000 is a bargain. You can usually find one for under that amount at most large swap meets, but it will no doubt be freshly primed. This is an excellent indication that the body underneath is less than perfect. In fact, it will probably be filled with body filler and will no doubt be missing many of the hard-to-find interior trim pieces, such as window frames. Cars can be found today that everyone overlooked years ago because they needed extensive repairs or were poorly restored or modified. Correcting a bad restoration will often cost a fortune. That $6,000 bargain '32 coupe body may cost well over $20,000 after the bodywork is complete and

Gibbon is one of the largest suppliers of fiberglass bodies to the hot rodding industry. Here, a '32 three-window body is being assembled on an original '32 frame at the Gibbon shop. A good fiberglass reproduction '32 body cost about half of what a steel body costs.

the missing parts are found. The best advice I ever received was to buy the absolute best body you could afford, because it will be cheaper in the long run.

One way to obtain a complete steel body coupe is to buy an older restoration. This is an excellent, albeit expensive, way to get a solid body with all the trim pieces. Many hot rodders have financed their project by selling off the unneeded components to those who are restoring a similar model. Turning a restoration into a hot rod is also an excellent way to make enemies within the restoration community. Restorers hate to see hot rods evolve from a fully restored car or an original car that is worthy of restoration. Financially, a well-built '32 Ford hot rod will have a higher value than an excellent '32 Ford restoration.

An alternative to a steel deuce body is a fiberglass reproduction. Many purists turn their noses up at the thought of a fiberglass body, but it's an affordable way to get into a deuce coupe. Both three- and five-window body styles are available, with either a chopped or standard height roof. What's nice about ordering a "new" deuce coupe body is that the prospective owner can select

This Gibbon technician is assembling a mold for one of its fiberglass deuce grille shells. An original shell in excellent condition sells for approximately $1,000. A good steel reproduction sells for approximately $210, and a high-quality fiberglass reproduction can be purchased for $125.

from a long list of options. In addition to a chopped top, options include a recessed firewall, hidden door hinges, trunk or rumble seat, roll down or fixed rear window, a filled or working cowl vent, electric windows, and a tilt-out windshield. Most manufacturers of fiberglass deuce coupe bodies will do their best to suit every customer's needs, including chopping an additional inch or two on the roof, or adding a louvered steel deck lid in place of the fiberglass deck lid. Manufacturers can also add working door glass and door latches. Most manufacturers assemble the body on an original '32 frame or jig that is dimensionally accurate. Interiors of the bodies are reinforced with steel, hardwood, or a combination of both. A good fiberglass deuce coupe body can fool an expert into thinking the car is an original steel model. By the time the owner gets ready for paint, the cost of the fiberglass body will be about half of what a steel body will cost.

Another advantage of a fiberglass body is that it can be ordered with a chopped top of a standard dimension (usually 3 inches) at no additional cost. Changing the amount of the chop on a fiberglass body will cost additional money, but it will be far less than the cost of chopping the top on a steel body. Chopping tops on deuce coupes has been a tradition for over 50 years. It was initially done to reduce the amount of wind resistance for the coupes that ran on the dry lakes. Hot rodders also noticed that it improved the proportions of the car. An unchopped deuce coupe tends to look a little top heavy and boxy. When properly chopped, the roof and the body are more harmonious. An automotive designer once told me that the height of the roof should be only one-third of the overall body height. A deuce coupe with the 3-inch chop fits those dimensions perfectly.

John Guilmet has been building hot rods all of his life. This '32 three-window is his latest project. Guilmet fabricated a new lower rear panel, and he is in the process of finishing off the surface. Straight three-window bodies like this one are a rare find.

Chopping and Channeling

Chopping the top on a steel deuce coupe is one of the most distinct changes that can be made to the car, but it's not an easy task. It's a lot like getting a tattoo. Once the top is chopped, it's next to impossible to reverse the process. If it's done poorly, it's difficult to repair. Putting the saw to a 70-year old steel body is not a job for the faint-hearted or the inexperienced. Chopping the top on a '32 coupe is not as simple as cutting a section out and

welding it back together again. The windshield posts on both the three- and five-window coupes are laid back at a 10-degree angle, and the rear of the roof tapers slightly toward the top. It's like trying to take a cut out of the center of a funnel. The more that is cut out, the greater is the mismatch. There are two ways of fixing the mismatch. The windshield posts can be leaned back, or the roof can be lengthened. The experienced pros in the chopping business prefer to not lean the windshield posts

Some of the nicest hot rods come out of the So-Cal Speed Shop in Pomona, California. This chopped '32 five-window is being built for a customer. The steel body on this coupe is about as perfect as one can find.

back to solve the problem. Leaning the posts back creates an uneven surface for the windshield, resulting in a windshield that won't properly seal. The other alternative requires the roof to be stretched by the addition of a small panel to fill in the gap created by the front half of the roof that was moved forward and the back half that was moved rearward.

Before the first cut is made on a deuce coupe's top, a set of parallel cut lines must be scribed onto the surface of the roof and across the doors. These lines must be accurate, because a mistake of as little as 1/16 inch will be noticeable. In addition, the cut line must be stepped up to cut as close to the center of the rear window as possible, because the rear window is slightly higher than the door windows. The doors must fit properly before the sheet metal is cut, because fitting doors afterward is a nightmare. A power saw is used to cut the sheet metal, approximately 1/4 inch away from the line. Tin snips are used to get to the scribed line, and then the area is dressed with a sanding disc. A 3-inch chop in a '32 coupe will require the roof to be stretched 0.62 inch. This is done in an area over the door, where the section shape is relatively constant. This also means that the door frames must be stretched. It's critical that the door frames be straight so the door glass can travel up and down smoothly. Vertical slits are made in the A pillars and the rear of the roof so the surfaces can be aligned.

The process of dropping the body down over the frame rails is called "channeling." This five-window coupe has been channeled approximately 5 inches. (A '32's frame rail is 6 inches wide.) The typical channel is 6 inches, the width of the frame rail. Channeling gives the vehicle a lower profile without sacrificing ride and handling.

When chopping a '32 five-window coupe, the cut line is located above the upper door hinge. A three-window coupe has three door hinges, two on the body and one on the roof. To simplify the amount of work to be done when chopping a three-window, many will remove the upper hinge. Experienced customizers will keep that upper hinge.

Once the top is tack-welded together and the alignment is correct, it will be fully welded. The interior window moldings must also be cut and welded back together. The next task is to cut the windshield frame. A '32 windshield frame consists of an upper section that is U-shaped, and a lower section with a mitered corner where the two sections join. To cut the frame, cut the lower ends of the upper section and bolt the two pieces back together with new glass. The glass is flat on a '32, so replacing a windshield, or side or rear window is easy.

Channeling is another hot rod trick used to lower a deuce coupe. In the 1950s, channeling was very popular

Looking at the surface of this roof, it's hard to believe that it's been chopped. Expert metal finishing has eliminated the need for body filler. The roof has not been filled, so the wooden support structure for the fabric insert is visible.

on the East Coast and in the Midwest. A channeled car is one on which the body is lowered over the frame rails. On a '32, the body is customarily dropped 6 inches, because that is the width of the frame rail. A 6-inch drop is the most pleasing to the eye, because the bottom of the frame rail is in alignment with the bottom edge of the body. Channeling is easier than chopping a top, but it usually left to an experienced metal worker. When a car is channeled, the body is cut away from the floor. The body is then dropped down over the floor and frame rails and is reattached to the body. The rear frame rails must be cut to fit within the rear deck, and the firewall must also be cut to allow clearance for the frame rails. Chopping and channeling gets a '32 coupe about as low as possible. The only drawback is the lack of headroom.

Two other body modifications common to a '32 coupe are recessing the firewall and filling in the opening in the roof. Recessing the firewall entails moving the firewall rearward 2 to 3 inches. This is done to provide clearance for an overhead valve V-8, most of which have the distributor in the rear of the engine. A flathead-powered '32 can keep the original firewall location, because the engine is shorter than most overhead valve engines and its distributor is in the front of the engine. To fill in the opening in the roof and make it look correct, the panel that fills in the opening cannot be a simple, flat sheet metal insert. The panel must have a slight crown, or gentle curve, to blend with the natural curves of the roof. Many hot rodders will search junkyards for a station wagon roof as a starting point. An accomplished sheet metal worker can make a crowned panel from flat stock to fill in the opening. When a fiberglass deuce coupe body is ordered today, a recessed firewall is a no-cost option, and all fiberglass bodies come with a filled roof.

Interior

The inside of a '32 Ford coupe is cramped. Climbing into one that has been chopped, especially a five-window,

can be difficult. Suicide doors on the three-window makes entry easier, but anyone over 6 feet tall must make a few adjustments to drive in comfort. There was a sizable package tray in factory models between the seat and the rear window. Eliminating this tray gives the occupants an additional 6 inches of legroom. All '32 coupes were equipped with a comfortable bench seat from the

In this shot of the interior of the chopped five-window, the cut lines in the roof's sheet metal are barely visible. The wood around the windows provides a tack strip for interior trim.

factory. Most deuce coupe builders follow tradition and use the original bench seat or install one of the many aftermarket bench seats available. Leather, vinyl, and tweed cloth are the most popular upholstery materials.

One of the ways to create more interior space is to install a tilt steering column. Builders either modify a junkyard column or buy one of the many aftermarket tilt columns. Installing a smaller steering wheel is

another way of gaining more entry room. The most popular steering wheel in retro rods is the Bell three- or four-spoke sprint car-style wheels.

The list of deuce coupe creature comforts reads like an option list on a new luxury car. Today's deuce coupe owner can drive from coast to coast in air-conditioned comfort, with cruise control and a wide variety of AM/FM radios, tape players, and CD changers.

Rick Cronin, in red shirt, is a retired General Motors engineer who has been a gearhead all his life. His latest project is a '32 three-window coupe. The chassis is almost complete. The chopped body has been media-blasted, and a new recessed firewall has been installed.

Chassis

Once the body has been selected, it has to sit on a frame. Deuce rails are the only frames that look good under a '32 coupe body. The '32 frame rails have the characteristic "beauty mark" along the side that gives them a distinctive look. That beauty mark adds character to a '32 highboy. To be used for a hot rod, the original rails must be reinforced. This can be done by boxing, or welding a plate to the open inside of the C-section rail. For additional strength, a new center K-member is usually added. Many aftermarket manufacturers are making reproduction rails and complete chassis because of the popularity of the '32 frame. Everything from a bare frame to a complete chassis with independent front and rear suspension can be ordered. These chassis are categorized as Stage I, Stage II, and Stage III. A Stage I chassis is usually a bare set of rails with cross-members installed. A Stage II chassis includes the frame with mounts for the engine, master cylinder, and pedals added. A Stage III chassis is complete with steering box, springs, shocks, axles, brakes, and is ready to mount a body and install an engine. There's so much to say regarding hot rod chassis that several books have been written about them. Today's reproduction chassis are well engineered and safer than ever—a great foundation for any deuce coupe.

Tires and Wheels

Tires and wheels can make or break any car, especially a deuce coupe. The traditional look since the 1940s has been "big 'n' littles"—large tires in the rear and small ones in front. Dry lakes racers were the first to put larger rear tires on their cars, to effectively change the rear end gear ratio for a higher top speed. The larger rear tires fit within the deuce's rear fenders, and when run without fenders, it worked well with the proportions of the body. The look remains the same 50 years later.

Today hot rodders are using a wide mix of tires and wheels on deuce coupes. Car enthusiasts who are firmly rooted in the past lean toward bias-ply tires, but they have a wide variety of radials to choose from, including wide whitewalls. Before the advent of mag wheels, all that was available for hot rodders were wire wheels or standard steel wheels with hubcaps. The big 'n' little tire arrangement required wider wheels in the rear to accommodate the larger tires, and the trend in wheel size has followed the tire trend. Front tires that are too small and rear tires that are too big will tend to make a car look cartoonish. If they are both the same size, it will make the

Because of its simplicity, building a '32 Ford is relatively easy. With the body off of the frame, all of the engine and chassis components can be easily reached. This original set of frame rails has been boxed, and new cross-members have been added. The engine, transmission, gas tank, and full exhaust system have also been installed.

front of the car look heavy. There is no mathematical formula for sizing tires and wheels to a hot rod. The combination of chassis, wheels, and tires develop the car's "stance." Stance creates the car's attitude. When the stance is right, the attitude is right.

Engine and Transmission

In the 1940s and early 1950s, there was only one choice for a hot rod engine—the Ford flathead. It had evolved into a great powerplant and a lot of speed equipment was available. Not long after the first overhead V-8s were in production, they found their way in between a set of deuce rails. By the late 1950s, only the diehards were running flatheads. The new small-block Chevy was a perfect fit under a deuce hood; it performed well, and it was reliable and inexpensive. So long, flathead.

A wave of nostalgia has hit today's hot rod builder, and flatheads are cool once again. Parts are plentiful and modern engine building techniques have been applied to an engine whose production ended in 1953. Today's flathead is not as powerful as an overhead V-8, but it is reliable and just about the best-looking engine to ever sit in a deuce coupe's engine bay. It also has a sound that cannot be imitated.

The engine in Cronin's coupe is a small-block Chevy with a Corvette dual-four-barrel setup. The exhaust headers are rare set of Fenton cast-iron manifolds. Cronin has installed a four-speed transmission behind the Chevy engine.

Small-block Chevy engines have long been a favorite of hot rodders. They are the least expensive of all the modern V-8s because of the millions of engines that Chevrolet built. Dollar for dollar, it's easier to squeeze additional horsepower from a small-block Chevy than any other engines. Other hot rod favorites include any late 1950s and early 1960s Olds, Cadillac, Pontiac, or Buick V-8. In their day, these and the small-block Chevys, were the engines of choice for hot rods. Plenty of vintage speed equipment for these engines is available at swap meets, and some of the equipment is still manufactured today.

A wide array of V-8 engines can be bought in a box from the parts counter of your nearest new car dealership. These "crate engines" can be less expensive than rebuilding an old engine. They can also be purchased with more tire-smoking power than will ever be needed for a street coupe. With the exception of the Chrysler Hemi, all of these engines will fit under the unmodified hood of a '32 Ford.

There was a time when stick shift transmissions were the only kind of gearboxes available, and a '39 Ford transmission with Lincoln Zephyr gears was about the best gearbox anyone could have in a hot rod. In the 1960s, transmission technology took some giant leaps, due to the musclecar craze. The three- and four-speed manual transmissions that were being produced were stronger than ever. In the 1950s and early 1960s, an automatic transmission in a hot rod would have gotten the owner laughed off the street, but in the mid- and late 1960s, new automatic transmissions were being introduced that were stronger and more efficient. The energy crisis in the 1970s sent transmission designers back to the drawing board to create a new generation of

Look what I found in the workshop behind Don Garlits' Museum of Drag Racing! It's Don's personal '32 three-window under construction. Like most drag racers, Garlits was a hot rodder before he hit the strip.

One of the most gratifying aspects of building a deuce coupe is inviting friends over to help. Here, the owner (yours truly) is taking a break, while his buddy (fellow MBI author Dan Burger) wrenches on the engine.

The rake on Bruce Meyer's three-window is perfect. Correct body proportions, a well-designed chassis, and the proper big 'n' little tire combination make a great stance. One rule of thumb is to have the rear tires fit within the body's rear wheel opening and be concentric with the arc of the wheel house reveal.

The nose-down attitude on Elwood Peterson's black steel-bodied '32 five-window is achieved through a 5-inch dropped front axle and properly sized tires on American Mag wheels. The hood sides have been left off so everyone can see the blown small-block Chevy engine.

John Bade's '32 five-window was hot rodded in the 1950s. At that time the owner, in an effort to upgrade the ride and handling, installed the front and rear suspension from a 1956 Chevy. The front fenders have had blisters molded into the surfaces to provide clearance for the upper control arms.

The smiling man behind the wheel is Aaron Kahan. He owns this Buick nailhead-powered '32 five-window. Early Buick V-8s were one of the popular overhead valve engines in the late 1950s and early 1960s that were stuffed between deuce frame rails. Kahan is a member of the Choppers hot rod club of Burbank, California. This is one of a growing number of clubs devoted to preserving hot rodding's roots by building and driving traditional hot rods.

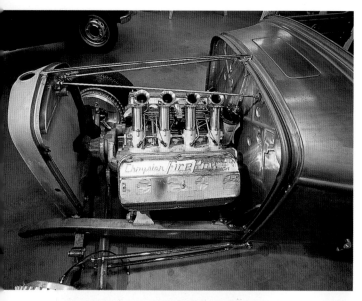

Left: The engine choice for a deuce coupe is subjective. Traditionalists like flatheads because they were the first hot rod V-8s, and others like small-block Chevys, because of their simplicity and low cost. This '32 coupe is being built with a vintage Chrysler Hemi, which requires a slightly recessed firewall. The Hilborn injection unit has been converted to electronic fuel injection. This hot rod will have the look of the 1950s with the drivability of a new luxury car.

Below: Flathead engines will always have a certain mystique in the hot rodding world. It was the first low-cost V-8 and therefore the first V-8 to be hot rodded. They were quickly replaced when overhead valve engines became popular in the 1950s. Today, many deuce coupe builders have returned to Ford's original V-8. A full-race flathead with three Stromberg carburetors on top is barely visible behind the front tire on Richard Lux's five-window.

Above: The itch to get into your deuce coupe and drive it is more than some owners can stand. Bill Webb's '32 three-window is far from finished, but it is drivable. It will eventually have a full set of fenders, and once the bodywork is completed, it will be painted black.

Left: Brent Bell's superstraight black '32 five-window has been built in a traditional style. It rolls on 16-inch steel wheels with small hubcaps. Bell has opted for a set of 1932 California license plates. Other details of note are a painted windshield frame, stylish curved headlight mounts with original '32 headlights, and a small "peep" mirror on the door.

highly efficient overdrive automatic and manual transmissions. Today, most hot rods are being built with these overdrive automatic transmissions, but there are a few diehards who will always feel that a real hot rod should have a manual transmission.

Details

Details make the difference between a deuce coupe that has been thrown together and one that has been carefully planned. The aftermarket is rife with traditional and billet accessories that blend well with the style of any coupe. Manufacturers offer several traditional choices for rearview mirrors, headlight mounts, and taillights on a deuce coupe. Accessories must blend harmoniously with the car's style. A bad choice will stand out like a pimple on a supermodel's nose. Hot rodders use the word "sano," a derivative of sanitary, to describe a car that has the right look. Correct body proportions, the

Jeff Vodden's chopped and channeled three-window is powered by a flathead. Holes in the quarter-panel reveal where the fenders once resided. Vodden and many other traditional hot rodders have turned back the clock by building and driving real hot rods, just the way they did in the 1950s.

right stance, and the many little details that round out the car characterize that look.

Hittin' the Road

Don Garlits once said of the hot rods of the 1950s, "When it runs, it's done!" Driving a deuce coupe, even if it's in primer or the interior isn't fully trimmed, is the best part of owning one. Most hot rods of the 1940s and 1950s were a challenge to drive, due to a poorly engineered chassis and marginal tires. They would dart from side to side, and they rode rough. Today's deuce chassis feature revised steering systems that eliminate bump steer and Panhard bars to reduce side-to-side sway. Today's reproduction bias-ply tires are a vast improvement over the tires of the 1950s and 1960s. These developments, with all the advances in engine and transmission technology, make driving a deuce one of the most fun things anyone can do.

Having a big blown Hemi engine doesn't stop Bob Berry, owner of this three-window, from racking up a lot of miles. Cars are made to be driven, and no car is more fun to drive than a deuce coupe.

Chapter 3

Five-Window Deuce Coupe Hot Rods

"Where were you in '62?" was the question that was asked in the promotional material for *American Graffiti*, a low-budget movie released in August 1973 that became one of America's landmark films. The subject was the cruising culture of the American streets, and the star of the show was a yellow five-window deuce coupe. *American Graffiti* showcased a number of actors whose future careers in films and television would become legendary, including Harrison Ford, Ron Howard, and Richard Dreyfuss.

American Graffiti was the dream come true of producer Gary Kurtz and George Lucas. Both were heavily involved in the selection of the cars that represented the

era. The '32 coupe was found in the Los Angeles area for $1,300. Kurtz was drawn to the coupe because of its chopped top. The car was full fendered and had been hot rodded, but to fulfill its movie role, it needed some extensive work. The film's transportation manager, Henry Travers, guided the car's transformation. Lucas' vision included bobbed rear fenders, motorcycle front fenders, and a chopped grille shell. The coupe was stripped of several coats of paint, and a fresh coat of Canary Yellow lacquer was added. The entire front end was chrome-plated and a fresh small-block Chevy engine was added. The engine had a Man-A-Fre intake with four Rochester two-barrel carburetors. Lucas also wanted a set of sprint car-style headers. The red and white interior was dyed black, and a pocket was added to the right door for the scene in which the coupe's driver, John Milner, (played by Paul LeMat) received a ticket for not having a license plate light. The frame was modified for removable platforms that would hold a camera, sound equipment, and as many as four production staff members to film the scenes set inside the car.

The '32 coupe used in *American Graffiti* was originally a full-fendered hot rod. The front fenders were stripped off, the rear fenders were bobbed, and a fresh coat of yellow paint was added. Like most movie cars, it has a few rough edges that are part of its charm and authenticity. Present owner Rick Figari maintains its drivability, but refuses to restore the car.

A pair of motorcycle front fenders were added to the *American Graffiti* coupe for early 1960s authenticity. It was during that time period that police would hassle hot rodders for not having fenders on their cars. Small motorcycle fenders became a popular addition. George Lucas requested the sprint car-style headers to give the car a more aggressive look.

Along with the '32 coupe, the staff had to prepare three other cars for the movie: a '58 Impala, a '55 Chevy, and the Pharaoh's chopped '51 Mercury. Today, when a movie or television series is made, several duplicate cars are available in case one fails, but the only duplicate car in *American Graffiti* was a second '55 Chevy for the rollover scene. One of the other challenges in the movie was to get actor Paul LeMat comfortable driving the coupe. He had to look as if he'd grown up in the car. LeMat drove in every scene except the final one, when the coupe and '55 Chevy raced on Paradise Road. Travers took the wheel for that one.

After the filming, Universal Studios felt that the movie would surely bomb and decided to sell off all of the rolling stock to recoup some of its investment. The coupe was put up for sale for $1,500 with no takers. The '58 Impala sold for $200. Universal decided to hang onto the coupe and leave it where sightseers on the studio's back lot tour could see it. Its engine and instrument panel were used for detail shots in another cult hot rod classic, *The California Kid*. The unexpected success of *American Graffiti* made those at Universal who decided to keep the coupe look like visionaries. The yellow '32 was dusted off, repainted, and

Above: Powering the *American Graffiti* coupe is a small-block Chevy with a Man-A-Fre four-carb intake. The engine was built more for its visual appeal than for horsepower. Twin master cylinders on the firewall control the brakes and hydraulic clutch.

Left: The *American Graffiti* coupe's interior remains the same as it was when the movie was filmed. The tuck 'n' roll seats were dyed black for the movie, but today some of the original red color is showing through. A pocket and some chrome trim were added to the passenger side door for the "ticket" scene. ("File that under 'CS.'") The famous piston gearshift knob is on the Hurst shifter.

The *American Graffiti* coupe's grille shell was chopped, and the front suspension was chromed for the movie. When the car was initially purchased for the production, the top had been chopped. When current owner Figari bought the coupe, the original movie prop license plates were in the trunk. The license plate, THX 138, refers to George Lucas' 1971 cult classic film, *THX-1138*.

rechromed for the sequel, *More American Graffiti*. Unfortunately, the sequel, like most sequels, failed to live up to its expectations. The coupe went up for sale in a sealed auction bid. The winner was Steve Fitch, who also owned the black '55 Chevy from the movie.

In 1985, Fitch sold the car to Rick Figari. When Figari first saw the movie, he was only eight years old. It was love at first sight for Figari, but he would have to wait 12 years before he could take possession. Figari's

first task was to make the coupe roadworthy, and he drove it a lot for the first few years. As Figari began to appreciate the historical significance of the coupe, he limited the driving and made the car available for shows across the nation. He even has his own website (www.milnerscoupe.com) devoted to the car.

It's gratifying to see that the most famous of all five-window coupes lives on. It's especially nice to know that the insidious bug of overrestoration hasn't

Alex "Axle" Idzardi's '32 coupe was built in the style of the 1960s. It takes many of its visual cues from Clarence Catallo's original blue three-window coupe, the original *Little Deuce Coupe*. These features include metallic blue paint, a chopped top with a white insert, and wide whitewall tires on chrome wheels.

The interior of Idzardi's coupe is trimmed in white and blue metalflake vinyl. Even the steering wheel and knob on the Hurst shifter are blue metalflake.

bitten Figari. The coupe's rough edges are still there, worn like a badge of honor.

Sparky's Black Coupe

Another five-window that was bought around the time *American Graffiti* was in production is owned by Mike "Sparky" Sparks of Glendora, California. Sparky bought the car in 1971 for $500. The man he purchased it from had owned it since 1952 and had driven it only twice since 1953. Sparky made the car roadworthy and drove it until November 1978, when he decided to rebuild the entire car. Like many car projects, this one sat until 1995, when Sparky's friends motivated him to put it together. In November 1999, Sparky drove his almost-completed coupe for the first time in 21 years. It lacked upholstery, a top insert, and hood, but it was roadworthy. In January 2000, Sparky trailered it to Howard's upholstery shop in Lake Havasu, Arizona, and in March, he drove it home to Southern California.

Sparky's five-window is powered by a stock Chevy 350 engine. The only upgrade is the Edelbrock aluminum intake with a 650 Holley carb. Behind the engine is a stock Turbohydro 400. The frame is an original Ford chassis that has been fully boxed and upgraded with a 9-inch Ford rear end and a dropped front axle. B.F. Goodrich radials are mounted on 1950s-era 15X7 wire wheels that are painted apple green.

Axle's No-Frills Five-Window

One deuce coupe owner who was heavily influenced by Chili Catallo's famous three-window was Alex "Axle" Idzardi. He wanted to build a '32 coupe that had the look of an early 1960s hot rod with the flavor of Catallo's *Little Deuce Coupe*. Idzardi is also president of the *Shifters* car club. The *Shifters* is the first of the clubs dedicated to preserving America's true hot rod culture. Their cars are rough by today's spit-shined standards, but are typical of the average hot rod that roamed the streets in the 1950s and 1960s. Their home-built simplicity and the lack of

From the rear, the nose-down rake on Idzardi's coupe is quite apparent. On the rear are 1953 Buick taillights, a vintage gold California license plate, and a *Shifters* club plaque.

Powering Idzardi's coupe is a 1960s era tripower Pontiac engine, complete with a chromed generator. The headers were custom made and painted white.

catalog-ordered billet aluminum components are a big part of their charm.

Idzardi's '32 coupe, like the cars of his fellow *Shifters* club members, is based on an original Ford steel body. It has been chopped approximately 4 inches. The only other body modification is a filled cowl, which was a

popular modification in the 1950s and 1960s. On the rear is a pair of 1953 Buick taillights and a *Shifters* club plaque. The metallic blue paint and white top insert pay homage to Catallo's coupe. Another early hot rodding trick Idzardi employed on his coupe was to paint the firewall white. In the 1950s, white paint was a low-cost

Sam Davis' '32 five-window was designed to look as if it had just rolled out of a 1940s hot rod time capsule. Back then, cars were built from spare parts and were driven with or without paint. Davis' coupe has been on the covers of both *Hot Rod* and *Rod & Custom* magazines.

substitute for chrome plating. Chrome is apparent on the front suspension, which features a dropped front axle and reversed eyes on the spring. The frame is fully boxed, and a Model A front cross-member helps lower the front end. Big 'n' little bias-ply whitewalls ride on 15X6-inch chrome wheels.

In keeping with the 1960s theme, Idzardi installed a tripower Pontiac engine backed by a Muncie four-speed transmission. The headers were handmade, and pipes from the collectors tuck under the frame to a pair of mufflers for street use. To maintain the retro theme, a generator was installed instead of an alternator. A pair

The top on Davis' coupe has been chopped a little over 2 1/2 inches, and the deck lid has been louvered. A 1940 Ford rear axle is equipped with a Halibrand quick-change center section. The taillights are 1939 Ford teardrop with blue dots.

of vintage Moon finned aluminum valve covers and a trio of chrome air cleaners top off the carpet.

The retro look continues inside, where pearl white and metalflake blue vinyl covers the bench seat. On top of the Izardi-built column is an NOS blue metalflake Ansen steering wheel. A Hurst shifter emerges from the blue-speckled engine. A fellow *Shifters* member donated a pair of 1960-era NOS clear blue metalflake floormats.

Idzardi and his fellow *Shifters* have started a trend in home-built no-frills cars. His '32 is constantly being worked on and enhanced, but it's also being driven as much as possible. To Idzardi and the *Shifters*, having fun means driving their cars and hanging out with their buddies. Idzardi's coupe harkens back to a day when ingenuity and hard work took the place of a Visa Gold card.

Sam Davis' Primer Five-Window

Sam Davis' '32 five-window also has a retro look. It also has the distinct honor of being on the covers of *Hot Rod* and *Rod & Custom* magazines. What's even more amazing is that his car is painted in flat black primer. These prestigious magazines know quality and style, and that's what Davis' coupe is all about.

While Davis was growing up in Southern California, the hot rodding bug didn't bite him until after he got drag racing out of his system. He first built a Junior Fuel dragster and then graduated to a Top Fuel dragster. His most famous ride was the twin-Chevy-engined *Freight Train*. In that car he won the gas portion of the U.S. Fuel and Gas Championship at Famoso Drag Strip in Bakersfield, California, where he ran a top speed of 207 miles per hour. After the drags, Davis' interest turned to European sports cars, but the road eventually led back to hot rods. "After going to the L.A. Roadster show for 20-plus years, it dawned on me that a hot rod of my own was what I needed," says Davis.

The car of Davis' vision was a 1940s-style coupe. In 1991, he started by gathering as many original parts as he

The red vinyl interior blends well with the red wheels and red grille insert on Davis' five-window. The shifter is attached to a '39 Ford transmission. An unpretentious rubber mat covers the floor.

Adhering to the 1940s theme, Davis selected a Ford flathead for power. Period-perfect speed equipment includes Navarro heads, a Mallory ignition, and a Thickston intake manifold with two Stromberg 97 carburetors. On the firewall is a beehive oil filter. A small alternator is hidden inside the original generator.

could find and afford. Some of the pieces he found were unusual and rare. For the engine, he found a Thickstun PM-7 dual carb intake; for the interior he located a rearview mirror with a clock, and a shift knob with an inset thermometer. Added to the chassis is a 1940 Ford rear axle with a Halibrand quick-change center. Other

swap meet discoveries include a pair of 1932 California license plates and four 16-inch-diameter Kelsey-Hayes wire wheels. Firestone bias-ply tires, 5.50s in front and 7.00s in the rear, are mounted on the wheels.

With the help of Scott Gildner, Davis chopped the top 2.6 inches. He also removed the drip rails and filled

Michael "Sparky" Sparks' '32 five-window appears to have been dipped in black lacquer. Apple Green wire wheels were an option on the original '32s, and the color combination still looks good today. The low front end is achieved through a combination of a dropped front axle, a Model A cross-member, and 195x60R15 tires. The only modification that was made to the body of Sparks' five-window is a filled grille shell and an added bull-nose trim piece. The stock headlight bar was replaced with a dropped version. Smaller-than-stock, 7-inch Deitz headlights were added.

the grille shell. Gildner added louvers to the deck lid and hood top panels. In addition to all that work, he filled a few bullet holes and then sprayed on the Dupont DP-90 black primer. The wheels and grille insert were painted bright red, with a matching shade of red vinyl covering the interior.

The only logical choice for the engine of a 1940s-era deuce coupe is the fabled Ford flathead. Davis' engine is a 1948 vintage with a 239-ci displacement. It runs a Winfield cam, Mallory distributor, and Navarro aluminum heads. The two Stromberg 97s that provide the fuel are topped with angle-cut chrome velocity

Stock '32 Ford taillights leave a lot to be desired. Sparks reduced the chances of having his five-window rear-ended when he added a strip of LEDs between the gas tank and lower body. They remain hidden in the shadows, and are visible only when illuminated.

stacks. Backing the engine is a '39 Ford transmission with Lincoln Zephyr gears. Davis does not like the unreliability of generators. An alternator is the best solution, but it doesn't fit the style of his car. Davis' ingenious solution was to hollow out the inside of the stock generator and slip in a Mitsubishi alternator. The result is 12 volts of reliable power and the correct look.

When asked to state the primary use of his deuce coupe, Davis simply said, "Fun." In addition to driving the wheels off this five-window, he's been on the River City Reliability Run, has taken it to the Antique National Drags, and has push-started a vintage Top Fuel dragster at the NHRA California Hot Rod Reunion. "I've drag raced, road raced, and ridden dirt

Above: Powering Sparks' coupe is a stock Chevy 350. The only modifications are the aluminum intake manifold and Holley carb. Valve covers are polished Corvette units and the Chevy ram's horn exhaust manifolds have been ground smooth and coated.

Right: Too many additions would have detracted from the simple beauty of Henry Ford's original design. A rearview mirror is a necessity for a car that is driven as much as Michael Sparks' coupe. Because of its smoothly curved shape, this rear view mirror is called a "swan neck."

Above: Shaun Price is the third owner of this '32 five-window. The body is all stock and all steel. The only modification is the dropped headlight bar.

Left: The interior of Sparks' coupe is trimmed in black Mercedes vinyl. Sparks built the steering column from 1 3/4-inch-diameter exhaust tubing. It's topped with a three-spoke Bell steering wheel. Stock window crank handles actuate switches for the electric windows. An air conditioner and CD changer are hidden between the seat back and trunk.

bikes, and I have a pilot's license," confides Davis. "But this car was gratifying to build and the most fun I've had with anything mechanical ever."

Shaun Price's Full-Fendered Five Window

Shaun Price takes the same approach to his '32 five-window as Davis—fun. Price's car was built to be a driver, and in the five years he's owned it, he has put on over 40,000 miles. Price is the third owner. The previous owner of his coupe had it for 35 years.

Above: The low stance on Shaun Price's '32 is due to big 'n' little tires and a 5-inch dropped front axle. In the five years that Price has owned the coupe, he's put over 40,000 miles on it. Air conditioning, leather seats, and a CD changer are comfort perks that have been added to Price's coupe.

Left: Part of Price's formula to make his coupe a solid driver was to install a simple engine. Other than a little chrome, the 305-ci Chevy engine in his coupe is unmodified. The small black cylinder on the firewall is the cruise-control module.

Originally built into a hot rod in the 1950s and then rebuilt in the mid-1970s, shortly after the film *American Graffiti* was released, John McClintock's '32 five-window has many of the features of the movie's famous coupe. Deviations include a body color frame, an unchopped grille shell, mag wheels, and a front-mounted Moon tank.

Price's all-steel rumble seat coupe is full fendered and very red. With the exception of the dropped headlight bar, the body is completely stock from bumper to bumper. Original accessory cowl lights have been, added along with a chromed windshield frame and second taillight. The car's noticeable rake is the result of a 5-inch dropped front axle and big 'n' little Michelin radials on 15-inch steel wheels. The rear axle is an 8-inch unit out of a Ford Maverick. Mustang disc brakes are in the front, with drums in the rear.

Price selected a 305-ci small-block Chevy engine to power his coupe. The only modifications are chromed Corvette valve covers and an aftermarket air cleaner. The transmission is a Turbo 400, which is also unmodified. Stainless exhaust pipes lead into a pair of Turbo mufflers for that hot rod sound.

While Price retained the factory cowl vent, he opted for air conditioning in his deuce coupe because of the number of miles he clocks and because he lives in Arizona. Adding to the driving comfort is an interior

In the 1950s, a Southern California high school auto shop class chopped the top and rolled the rear pan on McClintock's coupe. The taillights are from a 1941 Chevy with blue dots. Small nerf bars (bumpers), also made in the 1950s, are used on the front and rear.

trimmed in gray leather with a gray wool carpet. A LeCarra banjo steering wheel tops a tilt column, and a Pioneer AM/FM radio is wired to a CD changer for those special "road tunes." If that's not enough, Price has even added cruise control.

John McClintock's Yellow Five-Window Highboy

At first glance, John McClintock's '32 coupe looks exactly like the one John Milner used to cruise the streets in *American Graffiti*. It's a chopped yellow highboy with a Chevy engine, but McClintock's coupe first took shape long before the movie was made. When it was rebuilt in the 1970s, some of the flavor of Milner's car from movie was incorporated.

The furthest back McClintock could trace his car's history was to 1952, when it was a class project car for a Southern California high school auto shop. All the body modifications, including the chopped top and rolled rear pan, were done in that class between 1952 and 1954. It was also during that time that the black pleated Naugahyde interior was installed. In the late 1950s it was on the streets, full fendered and running an Olds 303-ci engine. In subsequent years, it changed hands several times, and it ended up in Michigan with brothers Craig and Bryan Smith in the late 1960s. In the early 1970s, they transformed the coupe to the state it's in today. There are some obvious influences from the *American Graffiti* coupe that can be seen, such as the color and multicarbed Chevy V-8. Since 1976, McClintock's coupe remains almost unchanged.

One of the unique aspects of McClintock's coupe is the piece of dark blue-tinted plexiglass used to fill the opening in the roof. It offers additional headroom, and the ability to see the sky. Another interesting interior feature is the chrome-plated dash panel with a woodgrain insert. One of the outstanding features, dripping with nostalgia, is the coupe's 327 Chevy engine. A vintage Edelbrock six-deuce intake manifold mounting Stromberg carbs tops the engine. The valve covers are also vintage Edelbrock with Moon breathers. Other vintage features to note are the nerf bars, front-mounted Moon tank, and Clay Smith "Mr. Horsepower" decals on the sides of the cowl.

The world of five-window deuce coupes is varied. Some are full fendered and others are stripped down highboys. Some use the latest in technology and others rely on time-proven engineering and vintage components. One thing they all have in common is that they're unmistakably cool and a blast to drive.

When McClintock's coupe was rebuilt in the 1970s, a 350-ci small-block replaced the car's vintage Olds engine. Edelbrock valve covers and a six-deuce intake were added. A polished firewall was very popular in the 1950s.

Chapter 4

Three-Window Deuce Coupe Hot Rods

In July 1961, *Hot Rod* magazine's cover car was a hot rod that redefined the way people looked at and built 1932 Ford coupes. That car was Clarence "Chili" Catallo's chopped and channeled three-window. It would soon become known as the *Little Deuce Coupe,* after it appeared on the cover of the Beach Boys record album of the same name. It was a car that evolved from a street-driven hot rod to one of America's premiere show cars.

In 1955, 15-year old Clarence Catallo worked at his parents' small grocery store in Allen Park, a blue-collar suburb of Detroit. In a gas station across from the store, he found a '32 three-window coupe for $75. He had a friend drive it home for him because he was too young to drive it himself. By the time Catallo got his license, the deuce was ready for the street. Initially, the car was

Mike Martin's yellow '32 three-window highboy was constructed to look as if it were built in the mid-1960s. Martin used one of Ford's rare single overhead cam (SOHC)427s for the engine. Steve Davis, one of the West Coast's top car builders, and several of Martin's friends, helped with the car's construction.

channeled, painted dark blue, and powered by a carbureted Olds. It had whitewall tires (dual whites in front) with black wheels and no hubcaps. Catallo took it to the newly opened Detroit Dragway and turned the quarter-mile in 12.9 seconds at 112 miles per hour. Like all hot rods in the 1950s, Catallo's coupe was constantly being changed, and he added more chrome with each version. One of the subtle touches added to the body was the raised rear wheel opening line. This seemingly insignificant feature made the bodyline follow the shape of the rear tire to create a smoother line.

The carbs soon made way for a McCulloch supercharger. Silver scallops were added along with chrome wheels. Catallo, who by now had picked up the nickname "Chili," as in "cool," took the car to Detroit's top customizers, the Alexander Brothers (Mike and Larry). They sectioned the channeled body and added three horizontal wings to each frame rail. They added a custom nose with vertically stacked quad headlights, and reworked the rear of the body with a rolled pan to match the grille. Chrome exhaust stacks that ended at the leading edge of the frame rail wings were added to

A Personal Remembrance

In 1956, when I was 11, I lived three blocks from the gas station where "Chili" Catallo parked his three-window coupe while he worked at his family's nearby grocery store. It was the first real hot rod I had ever seen in person, and I was crazy about cars, especially hot rods. Every day after school, I'd ride up to that gas station and hope the car would be there. If it was, I'd hang around for an hour or more and drink in every detail of the car. I secretly hoped the owner would come over some day and say, "Hey kid, want to go for a ride?" Unfortunately, I was never asked, and I could only dream of what it would have been like riding in that coupe. Then one day the car was gone, and I was too shy to ask the guys in the gas station where it was.

That car left a big impression on me. Every model kit of a '32 coupe I built as a youngster had aspects of Catallo's coupe. Now that I'm building a real '32 five-window coupe, it will also reflect influences from Catallo's coupe. When I saw the coupe on the cover of *Hot Rod* magazine in 1961, the blue three-window had dramatically changed, but I knew it was the car I had fallen in love with a few years earlier. When I was contracted to do this book, I knew I had to find that car. With a little hard work and a little luck, I was able to contact the late owner's son, Curt, and was able to reconnect to this piece of my childhood. When I finally saw the car again in person, a chill ran up my spine.

When Catallo was driving the wheels off this coupe in the late 1950s, his travels included this trip to the drag strip. His three-window coupe would run the quarter in the 12-second range. On the engine is a McCulloch supercharger; the exhaust headers consist of unattractive flex tubing. This photo was taken prior to the addition of the Alexander Brother's custom nose. *Author's collection*

the engine. Hubcaps from a 1957 Plymouth were added with white plastic flippers. The interior and top insert were done in white Naugahyde with blue buttons. One of the Alexander Brothers' trademark touches was a pair of dual recessed antennas, added to the coupe's left rear quarter, where they also doubled as the switches for the electric door solenoids. In the late 1950s and early 1960s, cars were regularly given names, and Catallo's coupe was called the *Silver Sapphire*. This Michigan car was ahead of its time, and even a step ahead of California's hot rods.

The draw of the West Coast was too much for Catallo, and in 1960 he and the *Silver Sapphire* moved to California. He took a job at George Barris' shop and

Clarence "Chili" Catallo bought this coupe for $75 in 1956. He constantly changed and upgraded the coupe. In 1961 it was selected to be the cover car for *Hot Rod* magazine and subsequently ended up on the cover the Beach Boys *Little Deuce Coupe* record album. ©*David Newhardt*

Above: The unique nosepiece on Catallo's coupe was designed and built by the Alexander Brothers, Detroit's top 1960s era customizers. The grille's horizontal bars were handcrafted and floated on a mesh background. The rare Kinmont front brakes are chrome plated. ©*David Newhardt*

Left: Catallo changed many things over the lifetime of the coupe, but he remained faithful to the Olds engine. Its final version was topped with a 671 GMC supercharger, three Stromberg carburetors, and a lot of chrome plating. The gold Barris crest on the side of the cowl was added following the 3-inch top chop at George Barris' West Coast shop. ©*David Newhardt*

A large 1950s era Lincoln steering wheel dominates the interior of Catallo's coupe. The coupe's cramped interior was trimmed in pearl white and blue vinyl.
©David Newhardt

swept floors, while he attended college in Long Beach. It was at this point that the final major changes were made to the car. Barris chopped the top 3 inches. Junior Conway added a new shade of blue to the car, along with white scallops in a pattern similar to the silver ones. Chrome wheels replaced the Plymouth hubcaps, but the wide whitewalls remained in place. The final touch was the addition of a 671 GMC blower and three Stromberg carbs. It was a magnificent car. Catallo's coupe was trendy, but it still retained all of the traditional hot rod components.

In 1961, *Hot Rod* magazine editor Bob Greene sent Eric Rickman to photograph Catallo's coupe. The images from that photo shoot ended up on the cover and in a four-page spread within the magazine. Another famous '32 coupe, owned by Andy Kassa of Passaic, New Jersey, was also featured in that issue. When Capitol Records was ready to release another Beach Boys album, it needed a car that would be perfect for the cover and that was a true "little deuce coupe." Capitol contacted George Barris and he suggested Catallo's coupe. The shot that was used on the cover was one of Rickman's outtakes. Shortly after the album's release, Catallo sold his coupe. He was a constant tinkerer, and he had done everything possible he wanted to do with the car.

Catallo's coupe spent some time in a high school auto shop, but remained nearly intact for 30 years. The

Olds engine had been replaced with a Mopar wedge, and the original frame had been scrapped in favor of a reproduction set of rails. In 1996, with a little urging from his family, Catallo bought his car back, determined to restore it to its former glory. Unfortunately, two years into the project, Catallo died of a heart attack at the age of 58. His son Curt was determined to finish the project in honor of his father. With his dad's gigantic scrapbook in hand, Curt was able to restore the coupe. In 2000, Curt Catallo drove his father's coupe out onto the lawn at the Meadowbrook Concours d' Elegance. Fittingly, the hometown favorite won the People's Choice award. The coupe has gone on to be displayed at the Pebble Beach Concours and at the prestigious Petersen Automotive Museum in Los Angeles, California.

Gary Moline's Flathead Coupe

Gary Moline's '32 three-window was inspired by another chopped '32 coupe that appeared on the cover of *Hot Rod* magazine in 1957. The car was a deep

Gary Moline's chopped '32 three-window was heavily influenced by a deuce coupe he saw on the cover of a 1957 *Hot Rod* magazine. The body on Moline's coupe is a fiberglass reproduction manufactured by Downs. It's chopped and has exposed door hinges and a working cowl vent. Contrast was added to the car by adding purple paint on the frame, rear wheel houses, and firewall. The color came from his granddaughter's crayon box. The wheels are polished American mags mounted with BFG Radials.

A single chrome push-bar protects the rolled rear pan of Moline's three-window. The taillights are 1941 Chevy with blue dots.

maroon '32 three-window highboy with a 5-inch chop that was owned by Lloyd Bakan. It had bobbed fenders in the rear, motorcycle fenders in the front, and a Chrysler Hemi engine. Moline always liked the car's overall proportions, the heavily chopped roof, and its clean looks. The vision of that car bounced around in his head for almost 40 years before he took action.

Moline didn't want to create a clone of Bakan's coupe, but he wanted to take its best elements for his own hot rod. When he finally decided to act on his vision, he added a few more changes that made the car more to his liking. Moline started with a Downs fiberglass three-window coupe body. Like Bakan's original coupe, Moline selected his with a chopped top. He also specified a working cowl vent, rolled rear pan, exposed door hinges, and original-style exterior door handles. For a frame and suspension he went to Total Cost Involved (TCI) for one of its Stage III deuce chassis.

Moline looked to hot rod tradition for his coupe's flathead engine. He started with a late block and bored it 0.125 inch over to increase the displacement to 276 ci. Ross pistons, Chevy valves, and a Winfield

286-degree-duration camshaft are located inside. Two other Chevy components were modified to fit the early Ford engine: a distributor and a water pump. All Ford flathead engines came with a pair of small water pumps that mounted on the front of the block. Moline mounted a 409 Chevy water pump, which has extended legs, to the front of the engine. At first glance, Moline's flathead looks like any other conventional V-8 engine with a single pulley for the water pump, but Ford never made a single pump for its flathead engines. The addition of the center mount, a single pulley pump, allows the owner to have various accessory drive options that would be impossible with the flathead's standard dual pumps. Moline's engine is topped off with a pair of polished Offenhauser heads and an Offenhauser intake with a trio of Stromberg carbs.

An 11-inch clutch that's attached to a Ford top loader four-speed backs Moline's flathead. Ford top loaders are usually shifted by mechanical linkage with arms that attach to the side of the transmission. When a shifter is installed in a narrow body like a '32 coupe, it ends up too far back and too far to the left and requires a unique shifter lever. Moline adapted a Jeep shifter that bolts to the top of the transmission. This positioned the shifter in the center of the car and as far forward as the original '32 shifter. Moline's Jeep shifter gives him the vintage look with the durability of a modern transmission.

One of the first things you notice when you see Moline's coupe is the two-tone paint scheme. Ten years ago he saw a '34 coupe that was under construction. Its frame was painted, but the body was in primer. Moline liked the contrast and decided to paint

Left: The underside of Moline's three-window is as clean as the top. The center section on the rear axle is a polished Halibrand quick-change unit. Coil-over shocks and a rear sway bar improve handling. The custom stainless exhaust system is completely polished.

his coupe black, with the frame and fender wells painted a contrasting purple. Finding the right shade was a problem, but Moline's granddaughter assisted him with the color selection. A crayon pulled from her crayon box was the perfect shade he was looking for. In addition to the frame and fender wells, Moline also painted the firewall purple.

One of the toughest challenges Moline encountered was how to comfortably stuff his 6-foot, 4-inch frame into the small coupe. Even without a chopped top, a '32 coupe can be a little confining for anyone under 6 feet. Moline removed the package tray, moved the seat all the way back, and lowered the seat as much as possible. He then added 2 inches of head room by tossing out the bows that support the headliner, and gluing the headliner directly to the inside of the roof. The result is a roomy interior for someone over 6 feet.

Moline's coupe is so clean, it looks as if it must sit in a garage between car shows, but it's actually a daily driver with over 11,000 miles on the odometer. Moline confides that even without air conditioning, the factory-style cowl vent keeps the interior cool.

Mike Martin's Cammer Coupe

Mike Martin's yellow highboy is another three-window deuce coupe with a Ford engine, but it's not a flathead. Martin opted for the Ford single overhead cam 427, one of the baddest engines ever built. Martin teamed with Steve Davis, one of the best hot rod/race car builders on the West Coast, to build his deuce. Along the way he got a lot of his friends involved. "Everyone who helped me build this car is a friend," says Martin. "It was very important to me that only my friends be involved in the process of building a car. It's such a long-term commitment that I wanted to have fun with my friends." It's obvious that Martin has some talented friends!

Martin wanted to build a 1960s-style car only using components that were available in the 1960s.

The flathead engine on Moline's coupe has been built for speed, durability, and good looks. A 409 Chevy water pump replaced the original flathead's twin water pumps. The distributor is also a Chevy unit, and an alternator is used for electrical system charging. Plenty of chrome and polished aluminum nicely dress the engine.

The 1932 three-window has always been his favorite car, and the SOHC 427 was his choice because that's what powered Jack Chrisman's 1966 Funny Car. The first three-window body Martin bought turned out to be in such bad shape that it couldn't be salvaged. The second body was much more expensive, but was in great shape and perfect for Martin's project.

Martin had Pete Eastwood stretch and box the original frame rails. Many deuce builders stretch the frame to increase the wheelbase from 106 to 110 inches. This subtle change helps to reduce the stubbiness of the car.

The profile of Martin's three-window is classic hot rod. The wheelbase has been stretched from 106 to 110 inches. This increase helps reduce the stubbiness of the coupe body and allow for an extended engine compartment. The blend of these elements is evident in the perfect alignment of the exhaust collector to the frame rail.

The frame was also Ced front and rear so the car could sit lower. The front axle has a 4-inch drop and the rear has coil-overs with ladder bars. Martin regularly switches between three sets of wheels and tires: Halibrand "kidney beans," Halibrand five-spokes, and yellow painted steel wheels with hubcaps and trim rings. All of the wheels in Martin's collection are 15X4 inches wide for the front

tires, and 15X10 inches wide for the rear. All front wheels mount 145X15 Michelin tires and all rear tires are 265X15 Continental.

Those who know Steve Davis believe he was born with a hammer and dolly in one hand and a piece of sheet metal in the other. He learned his trade by working with top-notch builders like John Buttera. When

Martin is asked about the work Davis did on his coupe his answer is "extensive." Most of the changes are so subtle that the casual observer will never notice; the cowl was raised 3/4 inch, the corners of the doors and deck lid were slightly rounded, and the A-pillars were leaned back 1/2 inch. The more noticeable changes include the chopped top—1 3/8 inch in front and 1 inch in the rear. The roof was filled, and a rolled rear pan was added. The top of Davis' custom hood opens clamshell style. The sides of the hood have blisters added to create clearance for the SOHC engine's valve covers. Depending on his mood, Martin runs the car with or without the hood sides.

Art Chrisman built the SOHC 427 engine. Ford introduced the SOHC engine in 1965 to compete against the Chrysler Hemi. This unique engine featured a pair of chain-driven camshafts, one on each Hemi-style cylinder head. The SOHC engines were made only for racing, and none were ever installed on the production line. NASCAR quickly banned them, but

Blue leather covers the interior of Martin's '32 three-window. The instrument panel has a small custom fabricated switch panel added, along with a custom steering column drop. The package tray has been removed so the seat could be moved rearward to add more leg room.

Ford's SOHC was released in 1965 solely for racing. This engine powered all types of drag race cars from gassers to Top Fuel dragsters. The timing chain for the two cams is over 6 feet long. Dual Holley four-barrel carbs rest on a polished aluminum intake.

NHRA and other drag racing sanctioning bodies allowed competitors to run them in Factory Experimental, Funny Car, and Top Fuel dragster classes. In addition to its excellent breathing ability, the overhead cam configuration allowed the engine to rev like a kitchen blender.

Martin's SOHC engine is equipped with a set of 9.5:1 forged pistons. The camshafts are stock Ford units, as is the crankshaft. Martin used a factory dual quad intake with twin Holley carbs, which was the same setup that was used on the Mustang A/FX racers. The ignition is a Vertex magneto. A custom set of stainless steel exhaust headers snake from the engine over the frame rails. When Martin turns the key, the

Beauty and function are combined in this Martin-fabricated combination headlight/shock mount. On most hot rods, these are two separate brackets that are built more for function than for form. Reversed spring eyes and a notched frame give the car a lower front stance.

big engine quickly rumbles to life. It has enough torque to gently rock the car from side to side when it idles, but it's docile enough to be driven in traffic. Behind the engine is a Ford C-6 transmission with a B&M 2,500-rpm stall converter. It's easy to hear the engine inside Martin's coupe because there's no radio or air conditioning. It's all hot rod deuce coupe.

Bob Berry's Hemi Coupe

Another three-window deuce coupe owner who likes big V-8s is Bob Berry. He started his deuce coupe project with only an engine. In 1995 Larry Holt of Speed Specialties built Berry a blown 392-ci Hemi engine. Berry has always had a fondness for Hemi engines. He installed a 331-ci Hemi in his first car, a 1957

Bob Berry's '32 three-window is based on a Wescott fiberglass body. Berry ordered the body from Wescott with exposed hinges, and he added a chrome windshield frame and exterior door handles to give it the look of an original steel body. The wheelbase was stretched 3 inches because of the length of the blown Hemi engine. The color is PPG Wild Orange.

Berry's coupe sits with a classic hot rod rake. The 15-inch diameter wire wheels mounted with big 'n' little radials have been painted silver. The taillights are '39 Ford teardrop with blue dots.

Plymouth Belvedere. In the 40 years since, most of Berry's cars have had Hemi engines, so it was no surprise to any of his friends when he had the Hemi powerplant built without having chosen a car. Once the engine was finished, he had to find a car in which to install it. "The '32 three-window coupe was a natural," quipped Berry with a smile.

Any Top Fuel driver would be proud of the engine Larry Holt built for Bob Berry. He started with a '57 Chrysler block and bored it slightly to displace 405 ci. To the stock rods, Holt added Aries 8:1 pistons. A Crower cam, lifters, and valve springs were installed next. Stainless steel valves were added to the stock Hemi heads. A polished BDS 671 blower serves two

Holley 600-cubic foot per minute carbs; a Vertex magne to bolted to the top of the engine provides the spark. Custom headers wrap outside the frame rails and connect to a pair of Ultra Flow mufflers. This combination is good enough to dyno 400 horsepower at the rear wheels.

Bob Berry selected a Wescott fiberglass chopped three-window deuce body and mounted it on a pair of Deuce Factory rails. Berry selected exposed hinges for the doors on his coupe, a chrome windshield frame, and stock door handles. These elements, along with the excellent proportions of the Wescott body, have fooled many into thinking it's a steel body. The car is painted Wild Orange. On the rear is a pair of '39 blue-dot taillights and a stock deuce gas tank.

The frame was stretched 3 inches to accommodate the big Hemi engine. Up front is a Magnum axle with a 5-inch drop attached to a chrome monospring. The 3.50 posi Ford 9-inch rear end is supported by Aldan coil-overs. Wilwood discs provide the stopping power up front, while 11-inch drums bring up the rear. Silver paint and chrome trim rings accent the 15-inch diameter wire wheels that mount big 'n' little radials.

Henry Arroyo did the stitching for the simple black Naugahyde on the Glide bench seat and door panels. The dash is filled with Stewart Warner Wings gauges, and the four-spoke Bell steering wheel rests on a tilt column. Berry's interior has all the comforts of any luxury car, including a Vintage Air air conditioning system, stereo cassette player, and power windows. The Lokar shifter connects to the Turbo 400, which has been modified with a B&M shift kit.

Bruce Meyer's Ardun-Powered Coupe

Bruce Meyer's bright red three-window highboy coupe also runs a blown "Hemi" engine of sorts. The engine is a Ford flathead with an Ardun overhead conversion and an S.CO.T blower—a rare beast. Meyer started with a full-fendered steel-bodied three-window

The big Chrysler Hemi engine in Berry's coupe is vintage 1957. It displaces 405 ci and develops 400 horsepower at the rear wheels. The supercharger is a GMC 671 with two 600-cubic-foot-per-minute Holley carbs on top.

Above: Zora Arkus-Duntov, the father of the Corvette, designed the Ardun cylinder heads on Meyer's coupe. Their hemispherical combustion chambers were a great leap in technology in the days prior to the mass production of overhead valve engines. The only new component on the engine is the finned supercharger manifold, which was made to look as if were cast in the 1950s.

Left: Bruce Meyer had his '32 three-window built to early 1950s specs. He started with a car that had been chopped and made into a hot rod. Meyer was drawn to the car because of its Ardun-equipped flathead.

Above: The interior of Meyer's three-window is covered in black vinyl. The seat belts are aircraft-style, and the steering wheel is a 1940 Ford Deluxe. Chrome window frames accent the interior.

Right: The instrument panel on Meyer's three-window includes the gauge panel insert that was included with the car. All eight gauges are vintage curved-face Stewart Warner units.

Howard Gribble's chopped three-window highboy has a stealthy look. The former owner of Halibrand, a company that makes mag wheels and quick-change rear ends, owned this coupe at one time. It was outfitted with Halibrand's best, which included a set of 16-inch-diameter knock-off wheels.

that had been hot rodded in the 1950s and 1960s. One of the reasons he bought the coupe was because of the supercharged Ardun converted flathead that was in the car. The Ardun cylinder head conversion for the flathead was designed and first built over 50 years ago by Zora Arkus-Duntov, the father of the Corvette. Ardun heads have a hemispherical combustion chamber that increases the engine's breathing ability and horsepower. Ardun heads were rare and expensive in the 1950s, and they're even more so today.

When Meyer got the car, the engine didn't run very well and the car's stance was all wrong. "Someone had just

The rear frame rails on Gribble's coupe have been bobbed, and a custom fuel tank has been placed inside the trunk. The rear spreader bar has a pair of built-in taillights, and a pair of '39 Ford teardrop lights are mounted horizontally on the rear of the body.

thrown Ardun heads on it and it didn't even run," says Meyer. "But when I saw the car, I knew it had the potential to be something that was real reminiscent of the 1950s." Dave Enmark of So-Cal Speed Shop reworked the engine. "When Enmark built the motor, I told him I didn't want a gun," recalls Meyer. "I want to put a lot of miles on this car, so build it as conservatively and as

strongly as you can." Enmark did his job well. Even with the blower, the engine starts easily and has a wide power band. The only newly manufactured part on the engine is the intake manifold, which was machined out of billet aluminum by Shane Wickerly of the So-Cal Speed Shop. The manifold has been carefully aged to look as if it were cast in the 1950s.

Above: From the size of the mail-slot windshield, it appears the front of the roof on Gribble's coupe has been chopped a little more than the rear. This is not an uncommon practice in the hot rodding world. The front brakes have Buick finned brake drums.

Right: Under the multilouvered hood of Gribble's three-window is a 350-ci small-block. Chevrolet ram's horn exhaust manifolds are used. These manifolds were used in the 1960s on Corvettes and passenger cars. Their simple design makes the installation of a small-block in deuce rails easy. Cast-iron manifolds are quieter and are not prone to cracking like tubular headers.

Other than the intake manifold, there isn't a part on Meyer's car that was manufactured after the 1950s. Even the unique gauge panel with its curved glass Stewart Warner gauges is the original one that was installed in the 1950s. "I have several roadsters, and I just thought it would be really cool to have a chopped highboy coupe," says Meyer. "It's never to late to have a happy childhood."

Howard Gribble's Halibrand Coupe

Howard Gribble's black three-window highboy also looks as if it had been built in the late 1950s. At one time, it was used in advertising for the Halibrand company. That's because the coupe was once owned by Barry Blackmore, a former owner of the Halibrand company. Fittingly, it is equipped with some of the most distinctive Halibrand components. The coupe's Halibrand quick-change rear end was among the best ever manufactured and it has a classic look that hot rodders love. Along with a quick-change rear end, Gribble's coupe runs authentic knock-off 16X5-inch "kidney bean" wheels on the front and 16X7s on the rear.

Gribble's coupe proves the point that a hot rod looks best when it's simple. He describes his no-frills approach to his deuce coupe as "a high-tech 1950s look." Without question, the louvered hood, filled grille shell, and classic hot rod Buick finned aluminum front brake drums exemplified the 1950s look. The interior is a pleated red Naugahyde with a Bell sprint car-style four-spoke steering wheel, and it has Simpson racing seat belts. Under the hood is a stock small-block Chevy. It can't get much simpler than that.

The milled stainless upper and lower control arms of the Kugel-built independent front suspension are visible under the fenders of Bill Lewis' three-window coupe. Lewis puts a lot of miles on each year, and he wanted an improved ride and handling.

The engine in Lewis' coupe is a 1995 Corvette LT4. With the exception of the exhaust headers and a little custom paint, the engine is completely stock. The accessory on the near side of the engine is the compressor for the air conditioning system. An electric fan is attached to the rear of the aluminum radiator, and the firewall is custom, with a recess for the engine.

Bill Lewis' Full-Fendered Coupe

At the opposite end of the deuce three-window spectrum is the coupe owned by Bill Lewis. He took a different approach when he built his all-steel, full-fendered three-window. Like most of the deuces in this book, it was built to be a daily driver. Since 1983 it has made five trips to the East Coast from California for hot rod events,

and it is a fixture at all West Coast rodding events. Between 1993 and 1995, Lewis completely rebuilt his coupe and made something good into something great.

Lewis added an SAC frame and Kugel polished stainless independent front suspension. The independent rear suspension is based on a Corvette unit and features Kugel's custom components. The front and rear disc

Late-model bucket seats were added to Lewis' coupe for driving comfort. An overhead console houses the CD changer controls. A leather-wrapped banjo steering wheel is mounted on a tilt column.

brakes are power assisted. The steering is a Kugel rack and pinion. Lewis' coupe has a suspension with no equal. The engine Lewis selected is a 1995 Corvette LT4 with electronic fuel injection. It's backed by a 700R4 transmission. The fuel injection and overdrive transmission provide a flexible combination that's both powerful and stingy on fuel.

Because Lewis puts on a lot of miles each year, he wanted to have the interior as comfortable as possible. Late model bucket seats are covered in a combination of leather and tweed. A wool carpet covers the floor. An overhead console controls the Panasonic sound system that includes a CD changer. A tilt column and air conditioning have also been installed.

Ford's '32 three-window coupe is a classic design, and hot rodders have taken advantage of its good looks and made it look even better. The distinctive suicide doors made the three-window a standout in Ford's 1932 line-up of cars. The three-window's timeless lines look great with or without fenders, and with or without a chopped top. The 1932 Ford, in any body style, will always be the icon for the American hot rod.

The personalized license plate declares Lewis' pride that his coupe is all steel. The taillight is a stock '32 unit with a built-in license plate light.

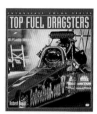

Top Fuel Dragsters
ISBN 0-7603-1057-2

American Drag Racing
ISBN 0-7603-0871-3

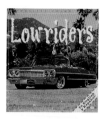

Lowriders
ISBN 0-7603-0962-0

The American Car Dealership
ISBN 0-7603-0639-7

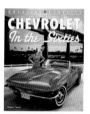

Chevrolet in the Sixties
ISBN 0-7603-0209-X

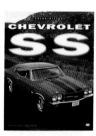

Chevrolet SS
ISBN 0-7603-0715-6

Vintage and Historic Drag Racers
ISBN 0-7603-0435-1

Hot Rod Nights:
Boulevard Cruisin' in the USA
ISBN 0-7603-0288-X

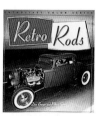

Retro Rods
ISBN 0-7603-0919-1